focus on asia

Korea

MATTHEW WILLIAMS

CONTENTS

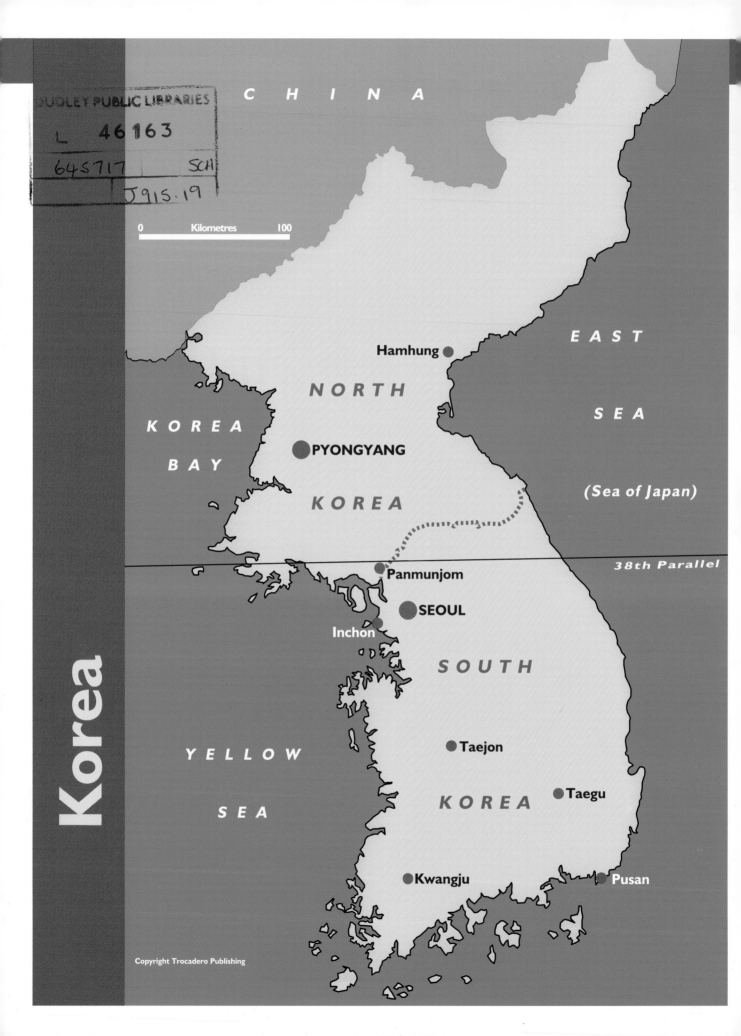

C H I N A

0   Kilometres   100

E A S T

Hamhung ●

N O R T H

S E A

K O R E A
B A Y

● PYONGYANG

(Sea of Japan)

K O R E A

38th Parallel

● Panmunjom

● SEOUL

Inchon ●

S O U T H

Korea

Y E L L O W

● Taejon

K O R E A

● Taegu

S E A

● Kwangju

● Pusan

Introduction to Korea

Korea is unique in today's world in that it is divided into two separate entities, both claiming to be the legitimate government and each with hugely different philosophies.

The Democratic People's Republic of Korea — commonly known as North Korea — is the last hard-line communist regime left in the world. It is poor, virtually bankrupt, and isolates itself from all but absolutely necessary contact with the rest of the world.

The Republic of Korea — commonly known as South Korea — follows a capitalist ideology, is mostly open to the rest of the world, and has, until recently at least, had a rapidly growing industry-based economy.

The partition of Korea occurred after World War II, when the peninsula was freed from Japanese control. Both the Soviet communist bloc and the Western Allies led by the USA sought control of the territory. In the turmoil of the postwar days, as a short-term method to calm matters down, the United Nations divided Korea into two zones of occupation. North Korea, which was designated as everything north of latitude 38°N, came under the Soviet Union. South Korea was placed under American control. When it became apparent there was no hope of reunification, in 1948 two separate governments were established. The subsequent Korean War cemented this division, which continues unchanged today.

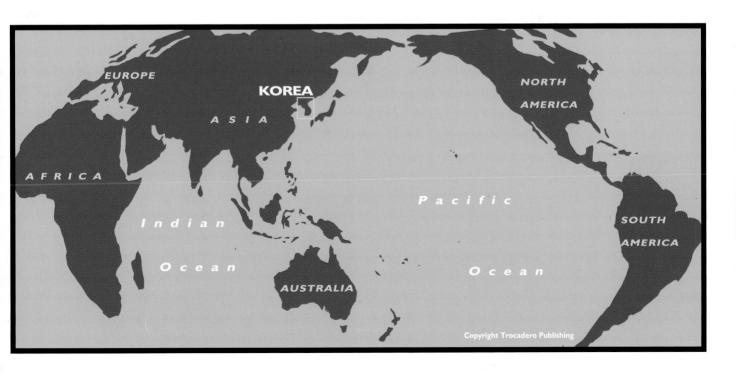

Government structure

SOUTH KOREA

Official name
Republic of Korea
Korean name
Taehan-min'guk or Han-guk
Government type
Republic
Head of state
President
Head of government
Prime Minister
Legislative branch
Unicameral National Assembly
Four-year term
Judicial branch
Supreme Court
Justices appointed by President
Legal system
Based on European and
Anglo-American law
with Chinese social structures
Administrative divisions
7 cities, 9 provinces
National day
Liberation Day — 15 August
(liberation from Japan, 1945)
Constitution
Most recent version adopted
25 February 1988
Voting
From 20 years of age:
non-compulsory, universal

NORTH KOREA

Official name
Democratic People's
Republic of Korea
Korean name
Choson-minjujuui-konghwaguk
or Chosun
Government type
Hereditary communist
dictatorship
Head of state
Chairman of the
National Defence Commission
Head of government
Premier
Legislative branch
Supreme People's Assembly
Five-year term
Judicial branch
Central Court
Justices elected by Assembly
Legal system
Based on German civil law
Administrative divisions
3 special cities, 9 provinces
National day
9 September
(foundation of nation, 1948)
Constitution
Adopted 1948;
revised 1972, 1992, 1998
Voting
From 17 years of age:
non-compulsory, universal

www.sources

www.korea.net
Official South Korean government site

www.cwd.go.kr/english
President of South Korea's official site

www.gksoft.com/govt/en/kr.html
Links to various government and political sites

search.asiaco.com/North_Korea/Government/
Links to North Korean government sites

NEWSPIX

North Korean leader Kim Jong II (left) meets South Korean President Kim Dae Jung for their historic meeting at Pyongyang on 13 June 2000

South Korea

South Korea today is essentially a democratic republic. The president is elected by the people. The National Assembly is also elected by popular vote for a four-year term. The original constitution that established the Republic of Korea in 1948 has been amended several times, not always for the better.

Today's relatively liberal South Korea is a great improvement on the past, especially for the ordinary citizen. The original leadership of Syngman Rhee was quickly replaced by a succession of authoritarian governments noted for their brutality and corruption. There were periods of military rule and martial law. The only compensation during these times was the rapid economic growth, which brought jobs and widespread prosperity.

North Korea

North Korea is the only hereditary dictatorship in the world; the only communist country in which the leadership passes from father to son. The Democratic People's Republic of Korea was established along Soviet lines in 1948. Initially with Kim Il Sung as leader, the communists — known as the Korean Workers' Party (KWP) — have controlled North Korea ever since.

The Supreme People's Assembly, whose members are elected for a five-year term, gives a superficial impression of democracy. In reality the country is very tightly controlled by the KWP. In common with other communist states, a personality cult was deliberately developed around Kim Il Sung. North Koreans were encouraged to see him as the Great Leader.

Transport

Public transport

Buses are the predominant form of public transport for most Koreans, in both the North and the South, as they go about their daily lives. Most cities and many smaller towns are well served by a network of bus routes, meaning virtually any location is accessible by bus. In South Korea there are usually two types of bus, local and express. The local is the one that stops frequently along the route.

South Korean taxis, especially those in Seoul, are very choosy about whom they accept as passengers and where they will take them. Would-be passengers stand on street corners and shout their destinations to drivers, who then accept the passenger they want. This has improved a little in recent years with the introduction of deluxe taxis, which provide a better standard of service. However, they also charge up to three times the fare of the normal taxi, making them unaffordable for many residents.

The South Korean cities of Seoul, Taegu and Pusan have underground railway systems, called the Subway. Mostly developed in the 1980s, they are modelled on Tokyo's super-efficient subway system. Trains are clean and fast, with air-conditioning to cool in summer and heat in the winter months. They serve a network of stations throughout the three cities, with each line being colour-coded to easily discern the routes and transfer points.

Long-distance bus services connect almost all parts of Korea. Most common are the inter-city buses, which have minimal comforts and are very cramped, but are also very cheap. Express and Deluxe buses offer more comfort and greater speed, but for a price. Travel by bus between cities and towns is popular in Korea.

Railways

The most reliable, fast method of travel from place to place in South Korea is by rail. Korean National Railroad's network connects major

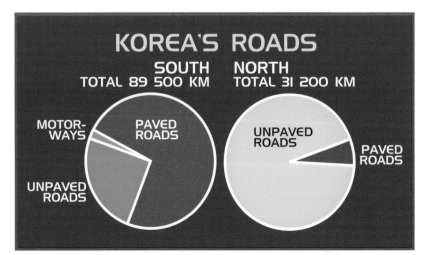

KOREA'S ROADS

SOUTH TOTAL 89 500 KM

NORTH TOTAL 31 200 KM

MOTOR-WAYS

PAVED ROADS

UNPAVED ROADS

UNPAVED ROADS

PAVED ROADS

centres of the nation, carrying large numbers of passengers and freight loads. The most travelled line is Seoul–Pusan, on which express trains run regularly throughout the day.

The first railway line in Korea was opened around 1900, developed by James Morse, an American. He used the European 1435 millimetre (4'8½") standard gauge, which was incompatible with that of Japan and other parts of northern Asia. The line, running lengthways down the country from the Chinese border to Pusan, was promoted as an extension of the Trans-Siberian Railway to Moscow. Japanese travellers crossed to Pusan by ferry, then joined the train for the journey to Moscow and on to other parts of Europe.

After partitioning in 1948, North Korea was left with the best of the railways, which still form a key part of its nation's transport network. As well as links within the country, express routes have operated since that time to link Pyongyang with Beijing and the Trans-Siberian line. There are no rail connections between North and South Korea.

Road

Roads in Korea vary from tiny lanes in the cities, never built for motor vehicles, to large and efficient motorways. Koreans drive on the right-hand side of the road. South Korea has one of the world's major vehicle-building industries so, unsurprisingly, the streets and roads are mainly populated by such names as Kia, Daewoo and Hyundai. Government policies protecting Korean vehicle builders against imports greatly aided the development of the motor industry. Road transport by truck is popular for certain types of goods in both North and South Korea.

An interesting feature of Seoul is its long road tunnels. These have been bored through the high hills that are part of the city's landscape to reduce travelling time between different districts within the city.

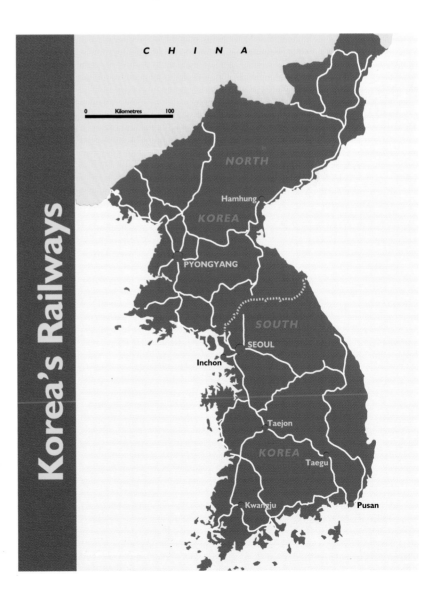

Korea's Railways

South Korea has a large fleet of ships specialising in carrying gas and petroleum cargoes

Aviation

In South Korea sixteen major cities are linked by the domestic airline services operated by Korean Air and Asiana Airlines. Because of the small size of the country, these are all quite short duration flights. Seoul is the main international gateway for

South Korea, with a large number of airlines flying to Asian and intercontinental destinations. Korean Air and Asiana also dominate the international routes. In March 2001 Seoul's large new Incheon International Airport opened for business, providing vastly upgraded facilities in comparison with the old Kimpo Airport.

Korean Air became embroiled in the Cold War when one of its Boeing 747s was shot down by Soviet Union fighters during the night of 31 August 1983. The aircraft, which was travelling well away from the usual approved route, was in the final stages of a flight from New York. As it overflew the island of Sakhalin, Soviet fighters intercepted it and shot it down. Many theories exist as to how this happened, but from today's vantage point it remains one of the needless disasters that marked the Cold War period.

Korean Air began life in 1948 as Korean National Airlines, with the government as its owner. In 1969 it was sold off to private enterprise, one of the first privatisations of an airline to occur. Most such sales occurred in other countries in the 1980s and 1990s. Through the 1980s it followed a path of aggressive expansion, opening many long-distance and regional routes.

North Korea's official airline is Air Koryo, which, until recently, was known as Civil Aviation Administration of Korea, or CAAK. Established in 1954, Air Koryo flies a small fleet of ageing Russian-built airliners from Pyongyang's Sunnan Airport. Its international routes reflect its part in the Cold War era, with services to

AIRPORTS	
South Korea	
With paved runways	68
With unpaved runways	34
North Korea	
With paved runways	39
With unpaved runways	48

Berlin, Moscow and Sofia. There are also occasional charter flights to destinations in Asia.

Shipping

While North Korea has its land border with China, South Korea is much like an island. With no traffic passing across the north–south border, all South Korean imports and exports must travel by air or sea. The large bulk of these go by sea, with the major port being Pusan in the south-east of the country. It is from here that a large slice of South

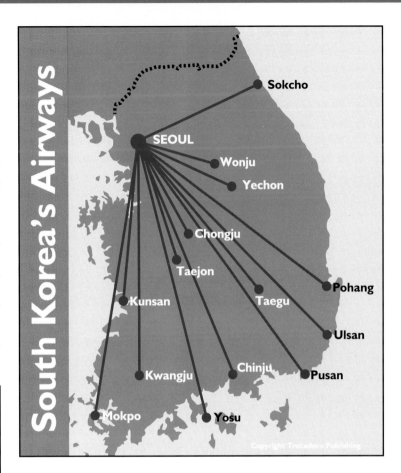

South Korea's Airways

Korea's manufactured goods are dispatched to markets across the world.

Part of South Korea's plan for economic growth in the 1960s was to develop a major shipbuilding sector. Today, Korean shipyards have achieved this objective with the capacity to construct some of the largest ships on earth, notably oil tankers plying routes from the Persian Gulf.

SHIPPING FLEETS

South Korea
Bulk 105
Cargo 168
Chemical tanker 38
Combination bulk 5
Container 49
Liquefied gas 16
Multifunctional large-load carrier 1
Passenger 3
Petroleum tanker 70
Refrigerated cargo 27
Roll-on roll-off 4
Short-sea passenger 1
Specialised tanker 4
Vehicle carrier 5

North Korea
Bulk 4
Cargo 94
Combination bulk 1
Multifunctional large-load carrier 1
Passenger 2
Passenger/cargo 1
Petroleum tanker 4
Refrigerated cargo 1
Short-sea passenger 2

WWW.SOURCES
www.koreanair.com
Korean Air official site

www.infoairports.com/asia/korean/
North Korean airports and travel

www.geocities.com/ichiban_jp/korea/
Links to many railway sites

Communications

Telephones

It is in the area of communications that the differences between North and South Korea are most glaring. For both fixed-line telephones and mobiles, South Korea has a huge penetration of ownership. Its telecommunications system is on a par with the rest of the developed world. North Korea, however, does not promote the ownership or use of telephones, and even if it did they would be prohibitively expensive for the average citizen.

South Korea is connected to the world via both submarine fibre optic cables and earth stations that use the Intelsat and Inmarsat satellites. North Korea's communications are mainly channelled by fibre optic cable through either China or Russia. However, it also has earth stations taking transmissions from Intelsat and Russian satellites.

Radio

South Korea is well served by both radio and television networks. One hundred and six stations broadcast on the AM band and ninety-seven on the FM band, and there are six short-wave stations. Such broadcasters are predominantly private-enterprise, commercial operators. Radio receiver ownership is the equivalent of one for every South Korean citizen.

By contrast, North Korea's broadcasting system is owned and very much controlled by the government. There are sixteen AM stations, fourteen FM stations and twelve short-wave broadcasters. There are around 3.3 million radio receivers in the country, vastly different from the South's 47 million.

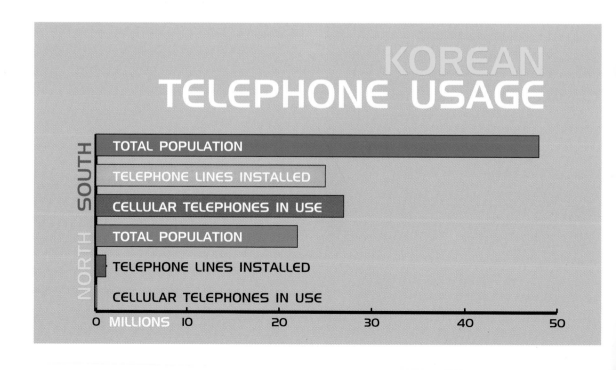

KOREAN TELEPHONE USAGE

SOUTH
- TOTAL POPULATION
- TELEPHONE LINES INSTALLED
- CELLULAR TELEPHONES IN USE

NORTH
- TOTAL POPULATION
- TELEPHONE LINES INSTALLED
- CELLULAR TELEPHONES IN USE

0   MILLIONS   10   20   30   40   50

Television

Korean television has a number of major networks transmitting programs through 121 stations and 850 repeaters across the country. South Koreans own around 16 million television receivers. In North Korea, as for radio, television is used primarily to disseminate state propaganda through thirty-eight stations. The number of sets is small, with one receiver for eighteen people.

Apart from the Korean-language operators serving the majority of South Korea's citizens, there is another substantial broadcaster: American Forces Korea Network. AFKN provides English-language radio and television programming for the many thousands of US military personnel and their families stationed across the country. With eight television stations, AFKN broadcasts a diet of US soaps, drama, comedy, news from home and current affairs, as well as information and special notices for the community.

Internet

Internet use is mostly free and open in South Korea. Its growth has been considerable, with around 15 million users logging on regularly. By contrast, in North Korea there is only one internet service provider, and it is controlled by the government. The North Korean level of usage of the internet is unknown, but thought to be minimal.

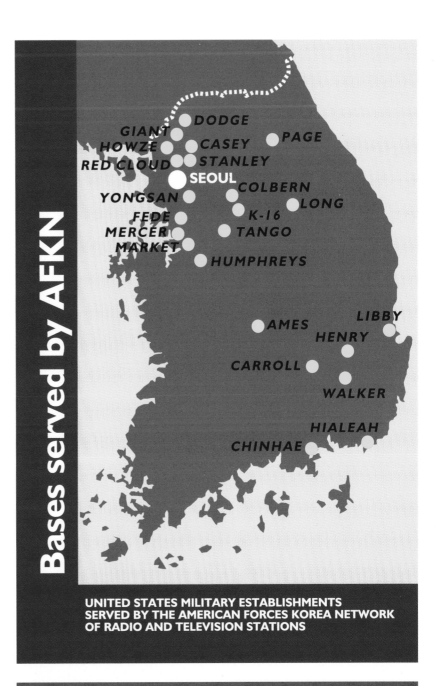

Bases served by AFKN

DODGE
GIANT
HOWZE   CASEY   PAGE
RED CLOUD   STANLEY
SEOUL   COLBERN
YONGSAN   LONG
FEDE   K-16
MERCER   TANGO
MARKET
HUMPHREYS

LIBBY
AMES
HENRY
CARROLL
WALKER
HIALEAH
CHINHAE

UNITED STATES MILITARY ESTABLISHMENTS
SERVED BY THE AMERICAN FORCES KOREA NETWORK
OF RADIO AND TELEVISION STATIONS

www.sources
afnkorea.com
American Forces media site
www.newsdirectory.com/news/press/as/kr/
Korean newspapers

Industry: primary and secondary

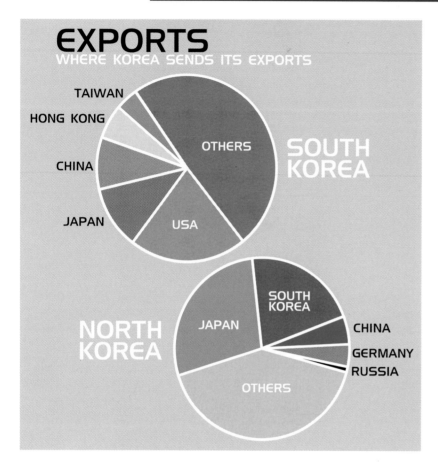

EXPORTS
WHERE KOREA SENDS ITS EXPORTS

SOUTH KOREA

TAIWAN
HONG KONG
CHINA
JAPAN
OTHERS
USA

NORTH KOREA

JAPAN
SOUTH KOREA
CHINA
GERMANY
RUSSIA
OTHERS

O pportunities for new ventures in agriculture are limited in both North and South Korea. The mountainous terrain leaves only twenty per cent of the total land area available for farming. Half of that is devoted to rice cultivation. Lower levels of fertility and bad land management have meant North Korea has had limited success with farming. At present the country is in dire condition, with widespread malnutrition and starvation because of crop failures.

The other major Korean source of food, especially protein, is fish. Fish and other seafoods are important in the Korean diet. Fortunately, the seas around the Korean peninsula are abundant producers of seafood. Even so, Korean fishers have begun ranging further afield, even into the southern hemisphere. The Korean fish catch is the seventh largest in the world.

Most of Korea's considerable mineral wealth is concentrated in the North, with iron ore, coal, gold, tungsten and graphite present in substantial deposits. The South has only ten per cent of the total Korean coal and iron ore reserves, which are vital to the development of heavy industries. In a bid to earn export sales, North Korea has substantially upgraded its coal and iron ore mining infrastructure. It also has substantial reserves of uranium, silver, lead, copper, zinc and manganese.

Heavy industry is a feature of the economies of both the North and South. When the Korean War ended in 1953, South Korea experienced a period of economic instability and shaky governments led by veteran politician Syngman Rhee. Following the 1961

KOREA'S EXPORTS
SOUTH KOREA
US$175 billion
Main products
electronic products, machinery and equipment, motor vehicles, steel, ships, textiles, clothing, footwear, fish

NORTH KOREA
US$520 million
Main products
minerals, metallurgical products, manufactures, agricultural, fish

KOREA'S MAIN SECONDARY INDUSTRIES

South Korea
electronics, automobiles, chemicals, shipbuilding, steel, textiles, clothing, footwear, food processing

North Korea
military products, machine building, electric power, chemicals, mining (coal, iron ore, magnesite, graphite, copper, zinc, lead, precious metals), metallurgy, textiles, food processing

KOREA'S PRIMARY INDUSTRIES

South Korea
rice, root crops, barley, vegetables, fruit, cattle, pigs, chickens, milk, eggs, fish

North Korea
rice, corn, potatoes, soybeans, pulses, cattle, pigs, pork, eggs

coup d'état that brought General Park Chung Hee to power, all the nation's energy was focused (often involuntarily) on industrial development.

A combination of protection against overseas competition and low wages paid to workers helped South Korea become a major exporter. In earlier years Korea's main exports were clothing and textiles. This has now given ground to heavy industry such as motor vehicles, ships, steel, chemicals and electronic equipment and components.

South Korea was severely affected by the 1997–98 economic problems that swept across Asia. Production levels were severely cut back and there were widespread redundancies among the labour force. While this has now been overcome, the economic downturn in the USA in late 2001 is causing further problems.

When Japan occupied Korea (1910–45) it established a number of heavy industries in northern Korea. Following partition in 1948 these were developed and expanded until the North was a major heavy industry player. Unfortunately, the collapse of much of the communist world in the late 1980s lost it most of its key customers. North Korean industry's rigid communist system limits the potential for developing non-communist markets. The North's principal manufactures are military equipment, machinery, steel and textiles.

A South Korean oil processing plant

www.sources

www.kcci.or.kr/kccinew/eng/default.htm
Korea Chamber of Commerce & Industry

www.kotra.or.kr/main/common_bbs/bbs_list.php3?board_id=34
Industry in North Korea

Geography, environment and climate

Korea is a peninsula extending off the north-eastern Asian mainland from China. Combining North Korea and South Korea, it is just under 1000 kilometres from north to south. To the west is the Yellow Sea and to the east is the East Sea as it is known to Koreans, or the Sea of Japan as it is more generally known. To the south the Korea

KOREA'S SIZE
Total area **218 590 sq. km**
South Korea
Area **98 190 sq. km**
North Korea
Area **120 410 sq. km**

Strait separates the peninsula from Japan; and to the north the Yalu River marks the border with China.

Korea is mostly a mountainous land with a series of ranges running down the eastern coast, the principal being the Taebaeksan Range. Mountains are separated by deep, narrow valleys through which often run short, unnavigable rivers. The western and southern sides of the peninsula feature wide coastal plains. The coastline is heavily indented, with more than 3400 islands of varying size in the offshore areas.

Korea's climate is one of extremes, from bitter cold in winter to considerable heat in summer. Although classified as a temperate climate, its geography tends to produce a number of unusual effects. It experiences the usual four seasons of the temperate zone: spring, summer, autumn and winter. However, during winter, the peninsula is heavily influenced by the Siberian air mass from the north, which brings severe cold and snow. In summer the predominant effect is from the maritime Pacific high to the south. This makes the land hot and humid. Mid-winter temperatures in Seoul range from -5°C to 5°C, while summer's range is from

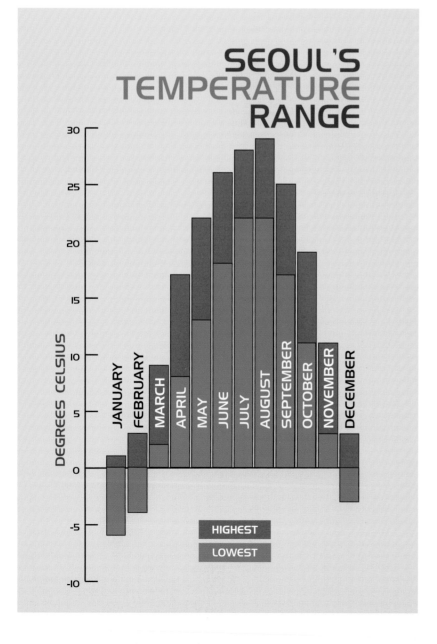

SEOUL'S
TEMPERATURE
RANGE

DEGREES CELSIUS

HIGHEST
LOWEST

KOREA'S LOCATION

South Korea
Latitude 37°N   Longitude 127°E

North Korea
Latitude 40°N   Longitude 127°E

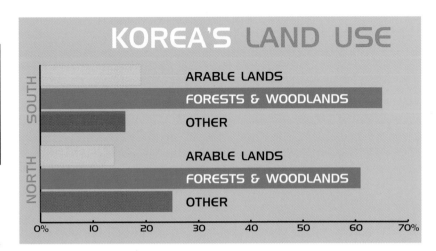

KOREA'S LAND USE

	ARABLE LANDS
SOUTH	FORESTS & WOODLANDS
	OTHER
	ARABLE LANDS
NORTH	FORESTS & WOODLANDS
	OTHER

0% 10 20 30 40 50 60 70%

20°C to 26°C. More than half Korea's annual rainfall is in the summer.

The effects of heavy industrialisation are evident in the environments of both North and South Korea. Heavy motor vehicle usage in the South has resulted in polluted air from the emissions. South Korea also suffers severe water pollution, mainly from industrial effluent and untreated sewage discharged into waterways. Acid rain, generated by the exhaust from coal-powered factories, is also a problem.

North Korea suffers less from industrial pollution problems and more from inadequate infrastructure. Even so, old-fashioned factories produce considerable air pollution. Poor land management has led to soil erosion and degradation, while water supplies can be polluted and diseased.

Mountainous country that is typical of Korea

WWW.SOURCES

geography.miningco.com/library/maps/
blnorthkorea.htm
North Korean geopgraphy, climate and environment

geography.miningco.com/library/maps/
blsouthkorea.htm
South Korean geography, climate and environment

www.asianphilanthropy.org/countries/
korea/environment.html
Links to environmental sites

KOREA'S ETHNIC MIX

CHINESE AND JAPANESE

KOREAN

The people of both North and South are overwhelmingly of a homogeneous Korean background. The evolution of the Korean people goes back more than 9000 years, with little input from other racial and cultural groupings. The strongest outside influence came from the Chinese and the Mongols, both of whom held sway over the Korean peninsula at various times over the centuries. While there was a strong ethnic Japanese population in Korea during Japan's occupation from 1910 to 1945, this had minimal effect on Korean culture.

Nobody knows for certain how the Korean language, which is unique to the Korean peninsula, evolved. Spoken Korean is most closely related to Japanese, although even then it has

South Korean military power on display

many distinct differences. The syntax is similar to Chinese; however, it does not use tones to discern meanings as Chinese does. Korean writings began 1300 years ago, but initially used Chinese rather than a distinctive Korean style. Hankul, the Korean phonetic alphabet, was devised around 500 years ago. For an outside observer, Korean script tends to be less complicated than that of Japan or China.

Baseball is hugely popular in South Korea

A neighbourhood bookstall in Seoul

the rest of the population. Non-agricultural work centres primarily on heavy industry, mineral extraction and military service. The state controls all aspects of daily life.

South Korea is vastly different, having a private-enterprise economy, although with some state intervention at various levels. The average South Korean works a full day Monday to Friday and a half day on Saturday.

Daily life varies enormously for Koreans, depending on which side of the 38th parallel they live. The average North Korean lives a fairly bleak life under an unrelenting communist dictatorship. Where once North Korea was fairly self-sufficient, today it is unable to feed its people. There is widespread starvation and malnutrition. Agricultural workers live in communities of collectivised farms. Everyone works to produce food for

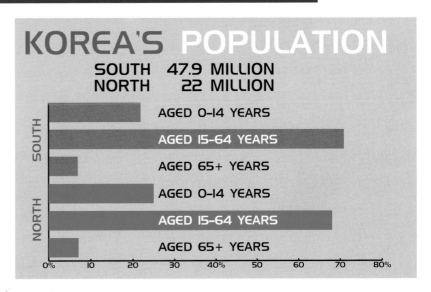

KOREA'S POPULATION

SOUTH   47.9 MILLION
NORTH   22 MILLION

SOUTH
AGED 0-14 YEARS
AGED 15-64 YEARS
AGED 65+ YEARS

NORTH
AGED 0-14 YEARS
AGED 15-64 YEARS
AGED 65+ YEARS

0%   10   20   30   40%   50   60   70   80%

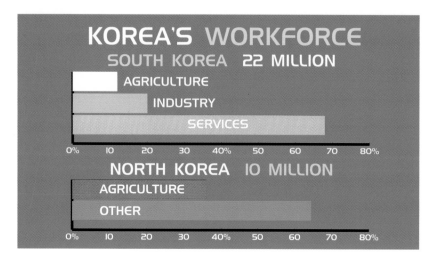

KOREA'S WORKFORCE
SOUTH KOREA 22 MILLION

AGRICULTURE
INDUSTRY
SERVICES

0% 10 20 30 40% 50 60 70 80%

NORTH KOREA 10 MILLION

AGRICULTURE
OTHER

0% 10 20 30 40% 50 60 70 80%

study, and to plan for three levels of education until they have attained a university degree. Students are taught in Korean, but most study English as a second language. While South Korea offers a wide range of higher education options, North Korea emphasises special skills and technical education. All Koreans, Northern and Southern, on reaching the age of eighteen years are conscripted to serve in their respective armed forces for a period of time.

While wages were kept artificially low in the 1960s and 1970s, they have now risen and created a strong consumer society, especially in the large cities. Travel to and from work is usually by subway or bus.

Koreans enjoy socialising with family and friends, although the extreme cold of winter tends to make theirs an indoor society for at least half the year. There are large shopping malls, suitably protected from the weather, that cater for most requirements from basic foods to all manner of consumer goods and entertainment. In central city areas there are large malls, full of small shops, built beneath the roadways to escape the winter cold.

Both Koreas encourage children to devote a great deal of time to

Korean women's national dress

WWW.SOURCES

www.moe.go.kr/english/english.html
South Korean Ministry of Education

www.knto.or.kr/english/ekorea/ekorea07.htm
Korean language information

Religion and beliefs

To the outsider, Korean religious structures can be confusing. While adherents to the Confucian faith are small in number, the ethical standards of Confucianism pervade all aspects of Korean society. This dates back to the early days of the Yi Dynasty 600 years ago.

The closest Korea has to its own religion is Chondogyo, combining various aspects of the Buddhist, Confucian and Tao faiths. Buddhism in Korea stems from the Mahayana line, having first arrived about 1700 years ago.

In South Korea Christianity is the dominant religion, despite being a late arrival to the peninsula. Over 200 years ago Jesuit missionaries working in China crossed into Korea, bringing

Confucian robes

their version of Catholicism to the people. Koreans' enthusiasm for the faith made the Yi Dynasty feel so threatened that a campaign of persecution was launched against the Jesuits. Protestant missionaries arrived in the 1800s, spreading their faith by practical methods such as establishing schools and hospitals.

Officially, North Korea has no religion as it is considered contrary to communist ideology. However, as was seen in other communist countries, this is no barrier to people retaining their faith. Buddhism, which can be practised individually and in private, is the strongest religion in the North.

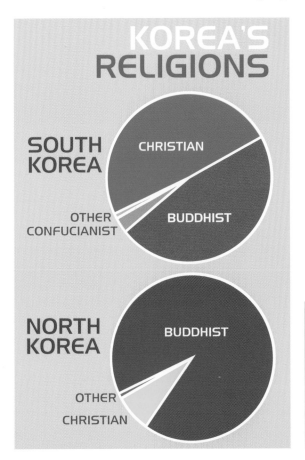

KOREA'S RELIGIONS

SOUTH KOREA
- CHRISTIAN
- BUDDHIST
- OTHER
- CONFUCIANIST

NORTH KOREA
- BUDDHIST
- OTHER
- CHRISTIAN

WWW.SOURCES

www.pbs.org/hiddenkorea/religion.htm
Guide to religions in Korea

www.asianphilanthropy.org/countries/korea/religion.html
Links to various religious sites

Arts, crafts and literature

Performing the classical Farmers' Dance

In 1861 a remarkable project was concluded by Kim Chong-ho. For thirty years he walked the country taking measurements and making drawings in order to produce the *Taedong Yojido*, a map of the country. Even today its accuracy is astounding.

Korean painting dates back around 1600 years to the murals painted on tomb walls to depict the deceased's life. At that time Korean painting was heavily influenced by China. Many artists studied in China, bringing its styles back to their homeland.

During the time of the Three Kingdoms, each had its own distinctive painting style. Those of Paekche and Koguryo tended to be more experimental. While the coming of the Unified Silla period led to a merging of styles, there was still considerable

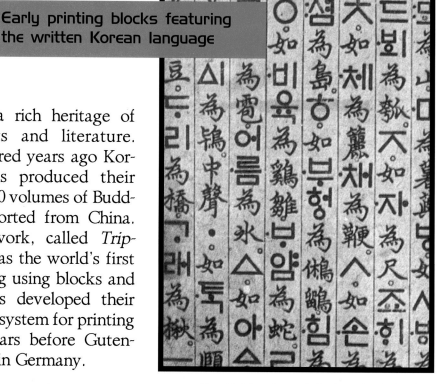

Early printing blocks featuring the written Korean language

Korea has a rich heritage of arts, crafts and literature. Nine hundred years ago Korean monks produced their own version of 6000 volumes of Buddhist scripture imported from China. This pioneering work, called *Triptikaka Koreana*, was the world's first example of printing using blocks and woodcuts. Koreans developed their own movable type system for printing more than 200 years before Gutenberg did the same in Germany.

input from China. During the Koryo Dynasty, from 918 to 1392, a school of religious art developed to serve the growing Buddhist faith.

The development of a distinctive Korean style gathered pace during the Yi Dynasty (1392–1910). The Silhak movement emphasised understanding based on actual observance of the subject. The Japanese occupation was a time of ruthless suppression of Korean culture. Little new development occurred until after liberation in 1945.

Over the thousands of years of Korean culture, the production of celadon has been prominent. Celadon, a delicate, translucent ceramic product, is finished in a blue-green colour. It is usually considered more valuable and precious than even Chinese Ming jade.

Korean performing art has its roots in Choyong, which developed in the later years of the Silla Kingdom. Not drama in the strict sense of the word, it was a collection of dances with dramatic storylines. A later evolution from Choyong was Sandae, which came into popular use in the Koryo Dynasty. While it mainly comprised dance, Sandae also featured actors speaking small amounts of dialogue.

Initially Sandae was performed for the king and his court, evolving into a more complex production involving specially written scripts. However, royal patronage fell away and it was taken up by the peasant masses. They loved the way it ridiculed the elites of Korean society.

After World War II the rise of cinema, and later television, as popular

A superb pottery jar from the Silla period

entertainments stymied further development of Korean drama. From the 1940s theatrical productions were restricted to small audiences in the main population centres. Changes began in the 1980s when younger people rediscovered theatre, with a number of experimental companies being set up, especially in Seoul.

Food and cuisine

Korean cuisine places high emphasis on vegetables and fish, and less on meat-based dishes. Rice, the staple diet for all Koreans, accompanies virtually all meals. Korean food, renowned for its highly spiced flavours, features ingredients such as red pepper, green onion, sesame, bean paste, ginger, mustard, soy sauce, vinegar, garlic and wine.

A full Korean meal, known as hanjoungshik, comprises grilled fish, steamed short ribs, meat and vegetable dishes, steamed rice, soup, and kimchi. Kimchi, uniquely Korean, is a range of vegetables flavoured with pepper and garlic. Pulgoki, which is widely known outside Korea, is barbecued meat cooked in a sauce of soy, garlic, sesame oil and sugar. Because of the bitterly cold weather, soup plays a major part in Koreans' eating habits, with extra spices added to enhance its warming effects.

Koreans use their own unique type of chopsticks for eating. They differ from those of other Asian cultures in that they are made of metal rather than wood. Western-style fast foods are making inroads into South Korea; however, Korean cuisine remains dominant for most people.

KOREAN FOODS

Kimchi Vegetables flavoured with pepper and garlic

Pulgoki Barbecued meat cooked in soy, garlic, sesame oil and sugar

Juk Gruel or porridge of rice or other grains

Guk or Tang Soups made from meat, vegetables, fish or other seafoods

Jjigae, Jeon-gol Stews and casseroles using meat or fish with soy sauce, soybean paste or red pepper paste added

Jjim, Jorim Dishes glazed with soy sauce or red pepper paste

Gui Meat or fish dishes cooked on a spit or grill

Hoe Sliced raw fish or meat eaten on special occasions

Jeotgal Preserved and fermented fish, clams or fish eggs, eaten as a side dish

Tteok Rice cakes cooked in a steamer

Namul Vegetables parboiled or fried with spices

Han-gwa Desserts and biscuits made of rice flour mixed with honey, eaten at ceremonies to honour ancestors

Hwachae Fruit drinks such as rice and cinnamon fruit punch

Cha Green tea, Job's tears tea, citron tea, ginger tea

WWW.SOURCES

www.lifeinkorea.com/
cgi-bin/menu.cfm
Guide to Korean foods

iml.jou.ufl.edu/projects/
STUDENTS/Hwang/home.htm
The story of Korean food

History and politics

Early civilisation

Korea's history as a distinct, unified entity goes back around 9000 years, with documented history commencing approximately 4300 years ago. It is claimed a Chinese scholar established a colony, where Pyongyang is located, 3200 years ago. It is generally accepted that migrants began arriving from other parts of Asia around this time, exerting considerable cultural influence on Korean tribes for 1000 years.

About 2100 years ago Chinese forces invaded. Thirty years later they were ejected from Korea, leading to the rise of the Three Kingdoms of Korea. These kingdoms, along with China, put Koreans through many years of conflict as each sought to dominate the other.

Three Kingdoms

Within 200 years each of the kingdoms — Koguryo, Paekche and Silla — had risen to a position of strength. On the banks of the Yalu River, in the far north, the first distinctively Korean kingdom, Koguryo, evolved. Silla and Paekche established their strongholds in the southern part of the peninsula.

From the first to the fifth century AD the Three Kingdoms were in constant conflict with one another. Finally, in the seventh century, Silla allied with China to conquer Koguryo and Paekche.

THE THREE KINGDOMS
Koguryo
Paekche
Silla

The United Silla

This period, known as the United Silla, saw relative peace and a flowering of artistic activities. Buddhism had by this time become the dominant faith of Korea. However, while it remained the state religion, Confucianism became the pattern for government and daily life.

In 935 Wang Kon peacefully ended the Silla era to found his own Koryo Dynasty. Everything went along reasonably peacefully for about three centuries, until 1231, when Mongol armies invaded, sparking off a thirty-year war. The result was a Mongol–Koryo alliance that lasted until 1392, when it was overthrown by Yi Songgye with Chinese aid.

Seoul's historic Bell Pavilion

SCOTT BRODIE

Colonisation

When Japan went to war with Russia in 1904, Korea had no choice but to let Japanese troops use its peninsula as a route into Manchuria. China was greatly weakened and could no longer come to Korea's aid. When Japan unexpectedly defeated Russia it kept its troops in place, declaring Korea a protectorate in 1905. Full annexation as a colony in 1910 ended the Yi Dynasty.

Korea both suffered and benefited under Japanese control. The old feudal kingdom was linked by a network of railways, communications were upgraded, modern factories were constructed and wholesale exploitation of rich mineral deposits began.

The Japanese were notoriously harsh. They regarded Koreans as second-class people who had allowed

The Yi Dynasty

The Yi Dynasty lasted just over 600 years, based at Seoul. Yi dumped Buddhism in favour of Confucianism as the official religion. A phonetic alphabet was developed and printing presses invented.

In 1592 the Kingdom of Japan invaded Korea. The invader Hideyoshi instituted a six-year conflict that saw incredible destruction and killing. Eventually, aided by China, the Koreans triumphed. Just over 100 years later, a much-weakened Korea fell to a Manchu Chinese invasion.

Hermit Kingdom

The following period of isolation lasted until 1876. Korea came to be known as the Hermit Kingdom, refusing any outside contact other than with China. Thus Korea was not infiltrated by Europeans as happened in other Asian nations.

In 1876 Japan forced change on Korea, and the Yi Dynasty agreed to a trade treaty. But, not wanting to be locked into a relationship with Japan alone, it signed trade agreements with European nations and the USA.

A large statue of Buddha in the Sokkuram shrine

two zones of occupation at latitude 38°N — the 38th parallel. Soviet troops occupied the north, Americans the south.

Two Koreas

The Soviet Union vetoed all UN moves for reunification and free elections. As Cold War tensions dramatically worsened, all trade and travel between the two zones ceased. The Korean economy was in chaos. The north had the industries and mineral resources, the south had the agriculture. Desperate Koreans tried to escape communism by fleeing south.

Finally, in 1948, two separate states were established: the Democratic People's Republic of Korea (North Korea) and the Republic of Korea (South Korea). All foreign troops were withdrawn from both countries during 1949. However, unlike the USA in the South, the Soviet Union ensured North Korea had a large, well-equipped army.

themselves to be conquered. Liberation groups worked to expel the Japanese, but they were weak and disorganised. A government-in-exile was established at Shanghai in China during 1919, led by Syngman Rhee.

A Cold War pawn

At the Cairo Conference of 1943, Korea was assured by the USA, Britain and China that it would become a sovereign nation when the war ended. Unfortunately the Soviet Union was not a party to this promise.

Following Japan's surrender in August 1945, against US opposition the Soviets moved to take control of Korea. To buy time for negotiations, the United Nations divided Korea into

South Korean soldiers in 1949, with equipment supplied by the USA

Outbreak of war

The crunch came on 25 June 1950, when North Korean troops crossed the 38th parallel into the South. The UN General Assembly demanded the North withdraw. President Harry Truman mobilised US forces, and the UN assembled a twenty-one nation coalition to defend South Korea. The grouping came under the command of World War II leader, General Douglas MacArthur.

The Korean War

Sweeping south, the North Korean army met little resistance from the much less powerful South Korean army and a small force of US troops. By 10 September 1950 the North Koreans had pushed their opponents into an enclave around Pusan.

MacArthur took retaliatory action on 15 September 1950, staging a highly successful landing at the port of Inchon, close to Seoul. The North Koreans, with their supply lines already stretched, began withdrawing. By 27 September they had crossed back into North Korea.

World war looms

At this point it was decided that UN forces would pursue their opponents into North Korea. China declared it would enter the war on North Korea's side if this happened. On 19 October UN forces captured Pyongyang, the northern capital. By late November, despite the bitter winter, they had reached the Yalu River, the border between Korea and China.

There was talk of invading China to depose the communists, but this was quickly forgotten when the UN forces saw the vast Chinese army waiting across the Yalu River. The Chinese stormed into North Korea, scattering the UN forces and using superior tactics to keep them on the run. By January 1951 the communists were in the South and had taken Seoul.

British soldiers going into action

A cold Cold War

Months of bitter fighting ensued, with Seoul returning to UN control in March 1951. Truman's refusal to let MacArthur once again invade the North led to a public feud and the general's dismissal. His replacement, General Matthew Ridgway, began truce negotiations, but the war dragged on for another two years.

President Harry Truman (right) and General Douglas MacArthur

After President Dwight Eisenhower threatened to use nuclear weapons, on 27 July 1953 an armistice was declared. Neither side had gained any new territory. The truce was signed at the village of Panmunjom, close to the 38th parallel.

THE UN FORCE

Members of the United Nations force that aided South Korea

Australia	Luxembourg
Belgium	Netherlands
Canada	New Zealand
Colombia	Norway
Denmark	Philippines
Ethiopia	South Africa
France	Sweden
Greece	Thailand
India	Turkey
Italy	United Kingdom

United States of America

Postwar Korea

Although there was never open conflict again, huge numbers of Chinese and North Korean troops remained in the north. Similar numbers of US and South Korean forces defended the south. South Korea today is a key base for the US military.

In November 1972 a formula for reunification talks was established; however, progress was very slow. The 1989 agreement permitted reunions between families separated since the 1940s. In 2000 heads of state from

A bridge destroyed by bombing on the Han River, near Seoul

South Korean leader
Syngman Rhee

North Korea remains a closed society. There is only very limited and tightly controlled inward tourism. North Koreans are not permitted to travel. All media is state controlled, ensuring the image of Kim Il Sung as the Great Leader is preserved.

When Kim Il Sung died in 1994 control passed to his son, Kim Jong Il. At the time of Kim Il Sung's death it was revealed that North Korea had developed nuclear weapons. While Kim Jong Il remains firmly in control of the nation, widespread crop failures and starvation may lead to unrest.

South Korea

South Korea's first president was Syngman Rhee, who had established the government-in-exile in 1919. South Korea, always the peninsula's agricultural zone, had no major industries and few natural resources. Unemployment was very high and inflation almost out of control.

both sides agreed to continue working on closer ties. At present, only the collapse of North Korea's regime would bring rapid change.

Industrialisation

Despite a large slice of its population fleeing south following the 1948 partition, North Korea embarked on an ambitious program of industrialisation. Aid money poured in from the Soviet Union, enabling railways and industrial plants to be modernised. All industries were nationalised and agriculture was collectivised in classic communist style.

Hard communism

When the Soviet Union and China adopted different paths in communism in the 1960s, North Korea played the two off against each other to benefit from their aid programs.

North Korean leader Kim Il Sung

Rhee's government struggled through the 1950s, weighed down by accusations of corruption and brutality. Following its re-election in March 1960, there were large protests about ballot rigging. When 125 students were shot by police, Rhee was forced from office and went into exile.

His successor — Chang Myun — had no more success. On 16 May 1961 the armed forces, led by General Park Chung Hee, seized power in a *coup d'état*. Freedom of movement and of the media were severely suppressed.

Military control

Despite the loss of freedoms, the Park government reduced corruption and industry was developed rapidly. Elected president at the 1963 elections and re-elected in 1967, Park placed South Korea under martial law in October 1972 to enable him to remain in office. On 26 October 1979 Park was killed by his own secret police chief. The new president, Choi Kyu-hah, increased the already tight martial law controls.

Economic developments

By the time of Park's death, huge amounts of foreign investment were flowing into the country. Labour unions had been brought under control, and low wages encouraged the establishment of factories.

On 12 December 1979 the military once more seized control in a *coup d'état*, responding to civil unrest following Park's death. Workers and students united in a popular uprising in Kwangju in May 1980. The military reacted with astounding brutality, killing more than two hundred protestors.

The South's prosperity is reflected in its bustling retail stores

In August 1980 Chun Doo Huan took over the presidency. By October another new constitution was in place. Martial law was lifted in January 1981. Chun's Democratic Justice Party won a majority in the National Assembly in March 1981.

New democracy

Pressured by the USA and others, Chun began releasing opponents from jail. The New Korea Democratic Party (NKDP) was formed by Kim Dae Jung and Kim Young Sam, two of the most prominent people released. At the February 1985 elections the NKDP became the main opposition.

In 1987, when Chun Doo Huan nominated former General Roh Tae Woo to follow him as president, huge protests broke out. It was possible the 1988 Olympic Games might be moved from Seoul. Roh gave in. A new constitution, with a directly elected president, was approved in October 1987.

SCOTT BRODIE

of the chaebol — Korea's family-controlled industrial conglomerates.

In 1996 former President Roh, Chun Doo Huan and thirteen former generals were indicted for the Kwangju massacre of 1980. Chun was sentenced to death — later commuted to life imprisonment — while Roh was sentenced to twenty-two years imprisonment. This victory for civil liberties was tainted in 1997 when both were freed under a presidential amnesty.

That same year Korea plunged into economic chaos as recession swept across Asia. The South Korean currency dropped fifty per cent in value, while the stock market crashed sixty per cent. Battered by the collapse and corruption scandals involving his family, Kim Young Sam was defeated by Kim Dae Jung in early 1998.

Reunification hopes

The new president, despite fierce opposition, agreed to an International Monetary Fund recovery plan. Distinct signs of improvement were evident by 1999; however, there were widespread retrenchments of workers. Non-performing divisions of the chaebols were closed or sold off.

One of Kim Dae Jung's primary concerns was the reunification talks. More than anything, it was Kim's 'sunshine policy' of the late 1990s that greatly increased the chances of a rejoining of the two Koreas. In June 2000 an historic meeting took place between Kim Dae Jung and Kim Jong Il of North Korea. Kim Dae Jung's efforts won him the Nobel Peace Prize in 2000.

A new era

In October 1991 a profound change occurred with the election of Kim Young Sam as president, the first non-military figure to occupy the leadership for more than thirty years. He immediately moved to curb the military's power and the economic power

WWW.SOURCES

www.koreanhistoryproject.org/l
Korean history

www.hawaii.edu/korea/bibliography/biblio.htm
Extensive historical bibliography and links

www.kimsoft.com/korea/eyewit.htm
History from a North Korean perspective

Statistics

Total population
South 47 900 000
North 22 000 000
Birth rate
South 14.8 per 1000 population
North 19.1 per 1000 population
Death rate
South 5.9 per 1000 population
North 6.9 per 1000 population
Infant mortality rate
South 7.7 per 1000 live births
North 23.6 per 1000 live births
Life expectancy
South male 71, female 79
North male 68, female 74

GDP growth rate
South 9%   North 3%
GDP per capita
South US$16 100
North US$ 1000
GDP by sector
South
agriculture 6%
industry 51%
services 43%
North
agriculture 30%
industry 42%
services 28%

Government revenues
South US$82 billion
North unknown
Government expenditures
South US$95 billion
North unknown

Labour force
South 22 million
North 9.6 million
Labour force by sector
South
agriculture 12%
industry 20%
services 68%
North
Agriculture 36%
Other 64%
Unemployment rate
South 3%
North unknown

COPYRIGHT TROCADERO PUBLISHING

SOUTH KOREA
Called t'aegukki, the flag's central symbol represents the yin (positive) and yang (negative) cosmic forces. It is surrounded by four trigraphs, one in each corner, representing heaven, earth, fire and water.

NORTH KOREA
The red star symbolises Kim Il Sung's traditions: the red stripe stands for patriotism and fighting spirit: the white bands represent Korean unity: and the blue symbolises world revolutionary unity.

Land area
South 98 480 sq. km
North 120 410 sq. km
Lowest point
South and North
East Sea — sea level
Highest point
South   Halla San 1950 m
North Paektu San 2740 m

Natural resources
South coal, tungsten, graphite, lead, molybdenum
North coal, lead, tungsten, zinc, graphite, magnesite, iron ore, copper, pyrites, gold, fluorspar, salt

Major exports
South electronics, machinery and equipment, motor vehicles, steel, ships, textiles, clothing, footwear, fish
North minerals, metallurgical products, manufactures, agricultural and fish products

Secondary industries
South electronics, automobiles, chemicals, shipbuilding, steel, textiles, clothing, footwear, food processing
North military products, machine building, electric power, chemicals, mining (coal, iron ore, magnesite, graphite, copper, zinc, lead, precious metals), metallurgy, textiles, food processing, tourism

Official language
South and North
Korean

Currency
South South Korean Won
North North Korean Won

Religions
South Christianity, Buddhism, Confucianist
North Buddhism, Confucianist

Index

Focus on Asia: Korea   ISBN 0 86415 427 5
Published by   Franklin Watts 96 Leonard Street London EC2A4XD
Created and produced by Trocadero Publishing   Copyright © 2002 S and L Brodie   Printed in Hong Kong